Pulse, Pressure, Pleasure

By: Ra'Mone Marquis

Pulse, Pressure, Pleasure
-Written by:
Ra'Mone Marquis

Copyright © 2023 by Ra'Mone Marquis
Published by Tru Phoenix, LLC .
Editor: Ra'Mone Marquis

Table of Contents

A Love Letter To Nun Ya Business

It's been a learning experience since I learned to release you from my mouth

There was an understanding I was lacking

There were times where you eluded me and I neglected you

Verbally we struggled while in writing we had a love affair

You helped guard me as you comforted me in moments of loneliness

Flushed

Divine

Evolution

You took me down a road of contentment mixed with your variations

You've helped me be strong

You've enhanced me

I've misused you but you've always sustained me

Significant

Bravo

An enigma of passion, pain, deceit, and joy

I've used you to inspire others while you healed me

I've used you to lead and guide

While you stood on the sideline always on time

You've helped me persevere

You've helped me take 3 steps forward when I was too afraid

to take one

I've used you to hurt others

I've used you for vengeance

You love me with remorse

You gave me resolution

I've received love in you

I've received healing from you

You've sunk me

You've helped me sore

At the right moment you've given me chills traveling through

an euphoric high

There's power in you

I receive power from you

You've opened doors for me

You took me into places of joy and peace

You've prepared me for a seat at the table

You've enriched my relationship with God

You aided me in having a peace that passes through to
understanding

Every second of the day you let me use you

I'm calmed by you in my sleep

Right moment...right time...right form

An unprecedented potential with undeniable variation joined
by intense need

An untamed usage meets eternal assistance

A muse

My mountain mover

My faith feeder

My silver lining and calm in the storm

You're my nucleus

My identity feature

Significant aspect to my existence

You, me, them...you are we and we are you.

An Ode To C

I admired you from a far

There was a presence that lingered

I was consumed by your softness and strength

I was intrigued by a gaze and smile

There's a favor and peace that comes from you

Something quite infectious is in your touch

Extra time was spent when the creator molded you

In your presence I'm made nervous and excited

Yearning

Joy

Thoughts unlimited

Your quality undeniable

Your voice commands me like 12 trumpets

While your words sooth me like the sweet sounds of Anita

Baker

Whether you bring me joy

Or have me caught up in the rapture

I'm digging on you

And these are my confessions

I'm so into you and I wanna be down

Jesus take the wheel

When can I see you again

You're makin' me high

If only you knew

You are my disturbia and I take a bow in your pleasures

I'm your baby tonight

I see we have something in common

Speechless

Say yes

Skin

Late nights early mornings

Whatever you like

I want to be the 808 to your 16 bars

The harmony to your melody

The rhythm in your R&B

The gospel in your soul

The choir to your praise

The modulation to your climax

Whatever you need me to be

With everything in you I see
The protector to your trust
I'd be your rock in a weary land
Your amazing grace on a cloudy day

Head Start

It clouds my mind and threatens my heart

It dictated my actions

It confused my judgements

It was long years past

Yet the touch is too familiar

The smell leaving remnants

I was young

No more hours beyond 6 years

Laid on the floor head on the pillow

It looked at me

The longer the daze the closer in distance I felt

New

Amateur

Confused

No answers

It crawled under my blanket

I didn't stop

Could I

Should I

It roamed my lower heaven

Caressing and moving in ways I'd never felt

I felt sting of sensation

Seasoned with fear and doubt

Marinated with curiosity and pleasure

I laid there mentally feeling as if I was unable to move

Multi tasked hands consumed my being

I became a prisoner to the touch

Violated

Embarrassed

But I liked it

Was I wrong

The touch changed from 10 fingers

To a moist fixture

I was tasted

Chills like a cold Georgia night attacked me with intent

I was lost

The ying demanded it to stop

The yang demanded it to continue

Conflicted

Unsure I laid there

Wrapped in a blanket of moisture and uncertainty

I was released upon

No blame

No accusations

With no hesitation or permission

With no talking or reciprocation

I knew then that I'd be searching

With no clue

No roadmap to find my answers

I look back and wonder if that was where it started

That moment wasn't the last

But the first of a journey unguided

Uncomfortable

Unfinished.

My Kind Of Love

It's an amazing feeling to love myself

I didn't achieve that at 15

And I was still lost at 25

I'm not a pity party and don't require sympathy

Love

Love is all I really wanted

Most of my life I hated myself

Never trusting myself let alone others

I searched for love in other's opinion

My validation came from the perceptions of others

Sex fed an ego and held a hold on me that made me numb

Not numb with pleasure

Numb with confusion saturated with no self-control

I just wanted a love where I felt special

Love that made me inspired and important

Acceptance...that's all I wanted from people

Later learning that others can't accept what I myself don't
respect
Anger, disappointment, resentment all handicapped me
I lost myself in other's needs and wants
Neglect...I did this to myself to a point where it became second
nature
I wanted a love where it was my days' stress release
A love that provides a peace and a solid rock
A love that gets me through my tribulations
A love that alleviates me through my flaws
A love that warms and comforts during life's cloudy days
Rather Ruby Dee or Ossie Davis, Will or Jada, Michelle or
Barack
I wanted and now need a love that's genuine, marinated with
respect
A love that's seasoned with trust
Accompanied with passion and baked with God
A love that stands the test of time
A love that ensures and strengthens
Infectious
Undeniable

Authentic with no force

The kind of love that Boaz had for Ruth

Or the kind that Luther sung about

The kind of love King Ahab had for Esther

Or the kind of love that Kobe had for the game of basketball

The kind that's patient and understanding

Love that mounts me on an eagle's wings

Stronger than a hurricane and as smooth as the wind

Both a camouflage and protector

Its supply never ends

Its range is limitless

Summed up together this is just simply my mind of love.

Sex Was Never My Healing

italicized words reflect those of Marvin Gaye not Ra'Mone Marquis

Marvin Gaye is my idol but I feel that he lied to me

I followed his guidelines

I obeyed the feeling

It was a feeling that chilled my senses and provoked my inner being

It put me to sleep one moment and energized me the next

I was lost and confused and I felt that it guided me

What a fool I was

Guess I was denied by its healing

Helps to relieve my mind

Sexual healing baby, is good for me

Sexual healing is something that's good for me

I've heard Marvin sing those words over and over

From childhood to adult hood I hung on to its every word

It has given me memories that haunt me

It has given me feelings that soothe me

Skills were perfected between the sun setting and the moon

rising

I yearned for it

I provided it in moments of desperation and bouts of truth or

dare

I'll be feeling fine,

You're my medicine, open up and let me in

I did

I was told to obey my elders

I felt more than fine

I felt amazing

Temporarily

I was guilty about it

I was pacified by it

I was crucified because of it

I was praised for its euphoria

When a touch can take you to an out of body experience

That is something to be cherished

When the taste of nectar is better than warm apple pie

Or more filling than grandma's table on Thanksgiving Day

There's a hallelujah that should be sung

A prayer that should be raised

I ran from it while I ran to it

I needed its power

I survived off its ecstasy

Whenever blue tear drops are falling

And my emotional stability is leaving me

There is something I can do…I know you'll be there to heal me

The love you give will free me

I want to be vulnerable to it

I want to be subdued by it….again

A healing I've seen but unable to be touched by it

A healing has visited me

As quick as I blink it is gone

Sexual healing knows my name but has abandoned my body

Judgement day and pearly gates is where I'll search

Marvin Gaye has some explaining to do

Maybe he'll visit me like a cool midnight breeze

And provide me with a cheat sheet or a short cut

Me and sexual healing have stories to tell

Me and sexual healing have a score to settle

With doors wide open and my window cracked
Sexual healing knows where to find me
Sexual healing has a purpose I'm ready to drive.

Wait On Me

I know it's a lot to ask

I may be selfish or I may be afraid

Hell I'm so confused I may be both

There's a fire that burns inside for you

Not the kind that burned down churches in the 90s

But kind that burned the bush that spoke to Moses

It's a fire that guides and instructs me

It draws me to you in ways that could defeat the strongest of

magnets

With you by my side I'm a mountain rooted in love

Saturated with compassion and support

Carved in a way that it can withstand any of earth's elements

There's a time in space for us that lasts forever

Prayerfulness led me to you

While a hopeless place entranced him

I'm subdued yet strong with your touch

Your presence inspires me more than Obama and Martin

combined

You provoke thought in me like Ghandi and Tupac

But wait

I have doubts and concerns

Not for you but for me

I'm flawed and guarded

I'm ready to move but fearful of pain

I don't want to hurt you and I don't trust me

Never having a good example of love

I've just learned to love myself

Forever isn't promised but with you it seems in reach

Is it my intuition or the devil knocking on my door

Can you wait for me?

I promise to love you like Langston loved poetry

Or how Louis love Jazz

How Jordan loved basketball

I promise to give you my heart on a silver platter marinated in

unconditional love and respect

But will you wait for me

My heart says I'm ready

My mind says stop

My heart says I've earned it

My mind says proceed with caution

Everything has a risk and with you I'm all in

With no life jacket I'm consumed by your sea

With no parachute I'm healed by your wind

Wait for me

Is it selfishness or fear

There's no cowardly in this lion

Fear has a battle it must lose

Wait for me

Wait with me

Grow with me

If it's you and me

That's the only thing left to help me be the best me I can be.

Moments With Intimacy # 1

You glance at me from across the room

It tells me your life's story

Spirits intertwined

Bonding over faith and tribulations

I'm entranced by you

You feel it too…

Rather over a NBA game or a Broadway play

We speak a language only we understand

Yet while saying nothing…

I'm caught in a daze

An intellectual high

Spasms of knowledge

Marcus Garvey to Obama

Slavery, Bus boycotts, George Floyd, Russia vs. Ukraine

Housewives, Power, Sportscenter, 911

You've experientially taken me on a ride

Soothing me without a touch

A journey, yet not moving

You learn that I love to exhale…we close our eyes

I taste the fire

From up close to 10 feet apart

All senses savored

Disruptions seized

This feeling we succumb to

Elevated

Euphoric

My inner me

Connects to our inner be

It has captured us…

Its name is…intimacy!

Deep Surrender

Hennessy and Mary Jane met among us
Laying the ground work
I'm in a daze
Dimly lit
Vanilla and lavender
Heightening a pathway untraveled
Ssshhh I feel it
A tingling chill dances through me
Captivating every sense
Taboo territory
I succumb to your control
Hesitant and excited
Your curved flesh teasing every desire
As your touch leads me
You test my flexibility
As you violate me in the best way.
Head spinning

Heart racing

Eyes rolling

I try to catch my breath

You tell me to match yours

Inhale, exhale, breath aligns with every thrust

I try to predict your next move

While holding back some of my own

Not too much

Not too little

As your body reacts I know to stay...right...there

Your breathing intensifies

A soft moan escapes your lips

I wonder how far you'll let me explore

As if you can hear my thoughts

You whisper, keep....going

This is an unmarked territory

Exhilarated because it's a fantasy fulfilled

Should I be ashamed with how good it feels

Limbs stretched further

My core is intensified

Veins pulsating

My strength matches yours

Your fingers follow a trail of nectar down my thigh

My tongue savors nectar

Flowing from your heavenly doorway

We're steps passed normal intimacy

Intense

Guiding me past my limits

Your craving escalated

Powerless and free

A hesitant pleasure moan flows from me

Satin pillow hides sight

My back arches as you…….

Enter

Gently at first

I test you

Your inner sanctum receives me

Deeper…. Harder…. Faster

Your muffled screams excite me

Passion dripping down my inner thigh

Warm…wet

I want more

Your body surrenders to me

Our rhythms become one

Your pleasure becomes my pleasure

Almost there

I retreat just as…

You explode on my tongue

And I drink

My thirst….is…quenched

-Written by Ra'Mone Marquis & *Arnique Craig*

Diamond

There was a chemistry we always had
Our eyes knew it
The gateway through which we met knew it
Two unknown paths
Two diverse stories
Two opposite sides of the tracks
Stuck
Curious
I was unattached
You had a situation of sorts
Game played
You knew where you wanted to be
Secret conversations heightened desires
We knew what we wanted to experience
Middle person's feelings would get hurt
So which one of us the 1st move make…….
…….At Randolph Street

Post-midnight

In bed minding my business

Text received from a mutual

My presence requested

No hesitations

I obliged

Minutes later inside the Altima I retreated

Our mutual in the driver's seat

In the back I joined you

An urban smell I highly enjoyed teased me

Black and milds

Side by side

Eyes communicating in the dark

You breathed into me

I inhaled your exhale

Elevated by a mixture

Cognac & Reefa

Certain hood mannerisms

No match for me

Defeated by our vibe

You surrendered

A whispered request to be devoured

Soothed my ears

Clothes holding you captive

I set you free

You're devoured

You're savored

Fresh chocolate and gyrations fed me

Smoke of Mary Jane

A cloudy companion engulfing us

Moans a symphony to my ears

Grip on my neck tightening

Bobbing and thrusting in sync

Expectation exceeded

Taste a salivating pleasure

Sexual IQ strong

An outpouring is near

Rhythms more intense

Our audience completely shocked

I crave more

As more is given

Deep in a zone

Extra lubrication and pool of protein

Inhabits my mouth

My esophagus its next location

Sensibilities overjoyed by a mission accomplished

Pleasantly buzzed

Tasting the cognac in your nectar

Services did your body good

Now my thirst is quenched.

Moments With Intimacy #2

No touching

No sticking

Spirit to spirit

Breath to breath

In sync

Connecting in a different realm

Passionate

Strong

Soothing

Calm

Five wicks feeding every sense

Vanilla, ginger, pineapples, lavender

Wax cascading down my chest

You placed your forehead an inch from mine

Electricity

Infectious energy blended

Eyes are locked

Anticipation

Control

Submissiveness

Our eyes have a conversation

Our lips can't translate

I wanna touch you

I wanna feel you

Restriction

Nervous and intrigued

We stay in the moment

The longer I don't take my eyes off yours

Hooked deeper

Entranced sustained

You exhale

I inhale

A euphoric high

You see my heart beating

My chest unable to hide it

It matches your rhythm

You trace my body without touching

Muscles tensed as your exhale feeds me more

Heartbeats match

Eyes locked glance to glance

You trace my body again…no touch

Face moved closer to mine

Slowly sucking out my breath

Before I could release it

Something left me

I'm overcome by a strong magnitude

Chills

Perspiration

My body traced again

Deep breaths taken…together

My frontal lobe caressed

Pierced right below my rib cage

My heart beat paused

Consciousness stuck

Cascaded by the five wicks

Something is yanked from me

A release

Strength deactivated

Tremors concerned me

Fluids drenched me
And your bosom welcomed me.

A Better Me Exists

It wasn't something I felt that I needed

Curiosity

Intrigue

Low self-worth

I ran from it

Didn't deserve it

Too much baggage

Not your responsibility

Self-sabotage

Like roaches from raid

I wanted you gone

Difficult

Every spray of something negative

Like a boomerang you returned

Loving me more and more

Fostering growth

Nurturing healing

Not wanting to hurt you

I pleaded for you to go away

Doubt

My own worst enemy

Denial

An unwanted sickness

My flaws intrigued you more

My walls became hurdles

You jumped easily

A game you easily won

My vulnerability mesmerized you

My heart made you captive

My stubbornness amused you

HE don't bless no mess

Your presence

A reason I surrendered

Your love became the calm after the storm

Soothing and alleviating chaos

Prayers, sensuality, consistency

Eliminating curses and sings that plagued me

Right amount of pressure applied

I'm elevated

Wounds closing

Success increasing

Fire of passion and joy…a guiding light

Rescued

A saving grace

Rather in your touch, prayers, food

Better me exists

Supported your words, actions, romance, and laughter

Better me exists

My courage

A muscle you flex

A little each day

Your presence

A reminder why with no one else

It had never worked

My serendipity

No accident

God placed you in my path

I sleep with the thought of you in my heart

You sleep with the love for me in your soul

This is why…A Better Me Exists.

This Is Our Love

Loving me harder than my insecurities

Loving me deeper than my deepest fears

I heard that's how it starts

When love conquers all

My body pleases you

My mind captivates you

My soul is where your deepest love resides

Connections with spirits intertwined

I wasn't looking for you

You weren't expecting me

Luck

Blessed

Favor

Simultaneously swept off our feet

You challenged every view I've had

Rareness

Two strong people coming together

Days where you're weak

I'm strong

Vice versa – no hesitation

Changes nothing

Find you sooner to love you longer

Few hours with you

Worth a thousand hours spent without you

Meeting you…..fate

Becoming friends…..a choice

Falling in love with you…..beyond my control

Deep devoted love

Present…..not just the pretty parts

Present…..no matter what

Just two hearts meant to be together

Nothing tearing us apart.

Go Easy On Him

Southern bread and fed

Broward county raised her

Curvy and vibrant

Ancestors are proud

The greatest of African kings exhilarated

Kitchen, boardroom, bedroom

Skills and talents undefeated and adored

Strong

Patient

Under construction

Beautifully flawed

Powerful

Her love cascading

A cold and rainy Georgia day

Intelligent

Sweet talker

No bullshit wasted kind of talkin'

She 'bout her business

She 'bout her man

She's a fool…..

Raw realness

Motivational and comedic relief

Unpredictable

Very essential

She's a fool…….

Get and keep not a problem

Her match met

She married him

A perfect match

Kansas City made

Midwest solid being with character

Patient

Open minded

Feeds the best parts of her

Soothes the complexes

Alleviation

A help meet

Her fun enhancer

Sexuality obliged

A whole vibe

He strums her perfectly

Flexibility not always a friend

Yet a hurdle she won't allow

Seduction her objective

She enticed heavily

Intentional with every move

She lured him

Like a spider to its web

High pleasure a goal

He no hesitation

Receives what's offered

Agency of his own

Desire vs. Desire

Flesh to flesh

Pleasure sounds a perfect song

Deeper in passion

Unprecedented experience of give and take

With every hole, movement, and parts

Engine tune up of sorts occurs

Body to body

Simultaneous

Control swapped

Flip flopped and shared

Intoxicated by brown spirits and euphoria

Sexual cha cha cha

A higher realm elevated

Remember she's a fool…..

Orgasm close

Skills not through

More tricks and treats to explore

Her body says, "Hell no we won't go"

Neck and shoulders a traitor

Pain destroyed euphoria

Not a nut released

Nor mission accomplished

Severe sprain

Body said no

Headed to ecstasy the goal

Laid out in the ER the outcome

No lies…no sugar coating told

Pleasure moans had created art

Cackling reigning through the ER

Simple message provided

Not one second adhered to

Nurse proclaims

Staccato tone through laughter

"Baby go easy on him next time!"

Nervous

Nervous

A lot of words flood my brain

The way your love has captivated me

Upgraded

Enhanced

Alleviated

Wrapped round and through me

Shackled with pleasure

Caressed with understanding

I get nervous

You walk into a room and my heart skips a beat

Chills when you touch me

Heaven when you savor me

Moonlight

Salivating a euphoric journey

Many times your servant

On a platter devoured and cherished

The eye rolling type of experiences

The late for work - family dinner cancellations type of

experiences

The increased heart rate numb in the legs type of experiences

Lips to lips

Have what you want kind of experiences

The skip the gym…cardio at home kind of experiences

I still get nervous

Never too tired

Mind's wheels always moving

Just wanting to lay my face in your lap

Feel your hand on my head

Remaining that way for all eternity

In every lifetime I'd find you and love you all over again

Thinking I needed someone to make me happy

Higher importance

You multiplied that

You create happiness around me

Your own happiness stimulates me

Our love

Obstacles and problems have been present

A team we are

Like the Showtime Lakers or Jordan's Bulls

Won it all consistently

We've pushed and pressed

On the other side we stand linked and connected like a chain

I still get nervous

We love each other deeper

The health… the love for ourselves sustained

You make me smile effortlessly

Not only telling me you love me

My doubts

You was patient enough to prove it

Nights when you're away

I struggle to sleep without you by my side

Love and connection so strong

A walk with you to the corner feels like heaven

You're not my first love, first kiss, first sight, first sex, first
date

But I want you to be my last everything

Loving you over and over forever

I still get nervous

Lost And Found

You touched me in a way

My heart didn't just skip a beat

Deeper

You reached the essence of my being

Nervous and denied

You reached through guards to the core of my soul

Used up

Temporarily unlovable

Not the right time

Team too much

Is this a location of settling

Each excuse each naysay

You burned with your passion

Undenied by your patience and purpose

You've allowed me to be myself

Loved me more for it

More than I wished for

Better than in my dreams

I don't doubt it

It's proven everyday

Lost was a place not taboo

A place which my contentment flowed through

I'd given up on finding it

Given up on envisioning it

Affirmed I didn't want it…devil's lies

Every road in the map of my heart

Leads me right to you

Not only letting me grow

You showed me how

Finding me by happenstance

You were like a lighthouse

Welcoming me home in the midst of a storm

You're not with me cause you need me

You're with me cause you want me

We've committed to lovin' it all

We've committed to lovin' our flaws

I look into your eyes

The rest of my life reflected back at me

Our love exists with a promise

To stay intact no matter what comes next

Face to face, flesh to flesh

More and more in love each day

Spirits intertwined

Your love has been powerful enough

Motivating me to become one with my soul

Emotional work to self-discovery and awakening achieved

You're my six word love story

I can't imagine life without you.

Committed/Love Loving You

Meeting you led to liking you

Liking you led to loving you

Loving you led to missing you

I did, I do, I will forever

Love loving you

One of my highest honors

Simplicity and complications

It's you I desire even more

Good mood

Bad mood

Petty

And handsome

You love me for exactly what I am

Days don't seem right without you

No matter location

I'm with you I am at home

Shocked

Humbled

Blessed

Never knew love would make me forget

That a heartbreak ever existed

I've acquired the one my soul loves

Love for you strengthened by

Million lil' things you never knew you was doing

It wasn't the butterflies in our stomach

But us building the garden in which they settled

Not perfect

I really love you

The deep, committed, genuine kind

Dedication

Your best friend

Your partner in crime

Your lover

In this life and the next

Forever.

The Abductor

She glows

Not in the freshness of her skin

But the joy in her smile

Sun kissed by the Caribbean sun

Honest and infectious personality

Confidence is high

Self-love good and solid

Tall, curvy, proportioned

The God's are pleased

Her objective – make a few tweaks

Wellness

Fitness

Led her to an unrequited destination

The abductor…….

The gym

Unexpected joy

Arousal

He was hired for a service

Training

Weight loss, etc.

The definition in his body had her in a trance

Dazed

She hoped to fit him as a glove

His shirts did

Fun banter

Flirting commentating

Provoked an after-hours kind of vibe

Accepted

Situation at home – no looking back

Gym vibe different

No longer shared with diversity

Her and him alone

No warm up needed

Body caressed

Shirts removed

He lowered himself

Eye to eye with her special place

Before a word could be released

An indulged appetizer

She became speechless

Moans harmonized with Usher in the background

Confessions

My way

In ways of Jodeci – she feened

Bewildered and lost with pleasure

Her control restricted

Feeling insane

Sweet and aggressive

Led backwards to sit

An unknown machine she's avoided

Stretches her inner thighs to the max

Bosom one by one getting TLC

Entered with force

Stroked with soft calm power

The abductor they call it

Each stroke by him

Her stretched bit by bit

Mistake made

She says, "It's been a while since I've been this open."

A positive trigger

Experience elevated

New positions introduced

Insanity roamed

Stars in the sky meet weakness

Numbness

Chills raced from head to toe

Deeper dug

Flexibility maxed

Back of abductor bitten

Eyes shut

Lost

Her scream erupted

Released from her like a volcano

Confused

Location unknown

Ecstasy ripped her of all consequences

Like cool down on a regular gym day

The floor mat met her presence

Near lifeless

She laid pleasantly violated

The abductor his throne

He eyes his handy work

Fully pleased and recuperated.

Rayda B's Love Notes #1

I smile like an idiot when speaking with you

Foundation for a dope love story

Falling for someone unexpected

Very unexpected time

Unexpected reason

You smile…

Stress is gone

Constantly reminding what butterflies feel like

No control where my love would land

Most sad, lost, broken period of my life

No falling in love 'cause of fun

It just happened

You being you…I know what love feels like

You saw the wars in me

Your choice? Stay, stand, and help me fight

You let me in

I found a safe place

Randomly smiling during the day

Always 'cause I'm thinking of you

You say I love you

Not to hear back

But to make sure I know

A chance you took

Make it worth it every day

One of my objectives

Luck and favor

Finding someone who feels good to my heart

I choose you

I'll keep choosing you

Over and over

No pause

Without a doubt

You are a part of my journey

The best part of this southern boy's story.

Rayda B's Love Notes #2

Used to not care to smile

You gave me a reason to smile again

The smile I have after each call

I just talked to the one that means the world to me

Can't get you off my mind

My mind always knows what my heart is thinking

You're my soul mate

A friend I can't stop kissing

A hundred lifetimes

A hundred words

A version of my reality

I'd choose you

I'd find you and I'd choose you

Dreaming of you even when I'm awake

You're my safe space and biggest adventure

Millions of folks in the world

Line 'em up…I'd still choose you

We didn't find love

We let it find us

We fell into it…

I mean it is called "falling in love"

We didn't force ourselves to fall

We just fell

How do we fit so perfectly

Jehovah custom fit us

I love the way you sound

Moan, yell, laugh

I embrace it all

Lovin' you past the moon

You're not near…I'm missing you beyond the stars

We hold when there's sadness

We kiss when there's crying

We laughin' when one's down

And loving' until we die.

Rayda B's Love Notes #3

They say it's best when it's a surprise

If I could live life over again

I'd find you sooner to love you longer

There's a strong feeling deeper than love

In you I could remain lost forever

You take away the blues

It's in your laugh

Your smile

How you make me feel

Which deepens my love for you

My heart talks about you constantly

I have been the exception to all your rules

You totally erased all mine

Unaware of true happiness and support

Taboo until I met you

We don't need fanfare or expensive restaurants

Happiness and enjoyment at a high

Me and you the couch our resting place

I text you 'cause I miss you

When I don't I want you to miss me

Everything 'bout you is my favorite

In a really good way you make me nervous

You brought new meaning to every song lyric I've loved

I wasn't sure when it happened

Can't tell you when it started

I knew right then I'd fallen hard

I could only pray you felt the same

By time my brain realized it

My heart had already fallen

I love your laugh when you can't control it

I love how your smile forms

When I cut up and you want to be mad but can't help but laugh

There's a strength in our foundation

We're dedicated to loving each other

When in the moments we not liking each other

I want all of you every day forever

I couldn't keep my eyes off you when I saw you

I couldn't keep my heart from racing when you smiled

You looked into my eyes

That's all it took for me to fall in love with you forever.

Glow And Flow

Swiped left and right

Tindr

Few interactions explored

Few experiences that passed the time

No maintenance handled

Advances denied

She had nothing on which to brag

She wanted to talk to the mic

She wanted someone to make it purr

Dry

Not her

The game that was thrown her way

Shots taken barely touching the rim

Then he showed up

Chocolate

Intriguing

Uninhibited

Wonderland

Night out visited

Spirits consumed

She watched him from her security monitor

Aroused with each step taken

She was mesmerized by how he glowed

His muscles enticed her as he got closer

Nervousness

Anxiety

Fresh smells of lavender and forest mist

Oils

Smooth skin

Dimly lit home

Cascading dreads

All she laid on display

Welcoming him into her dwelling place

His choice of clothes

Making him a glow in the dark creation

No time wasted

Height and strong back used sufficiently

Her 5'2 body suspended in hair

His face her resting place

Succulent and flavorful she was devoured by him

Gently placed on the kitchen counter

Sliding

Up and down

Counterclockwise motions

He experienced her in every way

Various motions of spread and dip teased

Her flexibility he quickly realized

In sync with rhythms

Intense passion activated

Thick lips sending chills up her spine

Helpless

Pleasure pains

Numb

Toes curled

Muscles tensed

A face ridden like life depended on it

Shirtless, still glowing, and in a zone

As if she was being turned out by something not of this world

He remained in control

She's a wanted guilty pleasure

Laid up on display in her own domain

He a doctor

His tongue examining every aspect of her body

Full checkup

Numbness travels from head to toe

Senses toiled with

Consciousness shaky

Her wrist restricted

She's tightly held captive

Unable to break free

Moans sore like sounds of a trumpet

Body jerks in diverse directions

Each jerk he devours her deeper

At last

Thrusts so strong

Digging done deeper

Moans modulate to a higher octave

Strong shoulders and cheek bones

He pulls out of her a release

A flood

The kind that reunifies you with a higher power

The kind that's transformative

Out of body

Forgetting her name and location

She's left on the marble of her kitchen's island

Basking in her nectar

Shaking uncontrollably

Slowly processing her euphoric high

He disrobed with each step towards her bedroom

Slowly climbing down

Clothed with concern, hormones, and excitement

Further into her domain she moved

Her knowing what's coming next

Not knowing if she was ready

Him not knowing what she's capable of.

1037

Brokenness and darkness captivated my life

Work and recluse a daily activity

Fire and desire my only objective

Silence the noises of life

I needed to

If only for one night

Or intermittent visits

Passion and pleasure needed to visit me

A higher sensual plateau with hormones and freedom…a must

Pre-conversation out of the way

We knew what time it was

No verbal communication

Our eyes told a story all its own

Aggressive

Passionate

Once the door shut there was no turning back

Built up energy

My body the storehouse

A release needed to occur

Body art

Pleasures to paint

Your body my blank canvas

You succumbed to every stroke, flex, and placement

Headboard gripped and dreads pulled

I devoured and savored you for minutes

Passionfruit, strawberries, and cream

You tasted better than the world's greatest aphrodisiacs

Replenishing me with each swallow

Transitioning inside of you with force yet respect

Your precious cargo fitted me like a glove

Your wonderland welcoming me – following my lead

No position taboo that night

Everything I needed to release you took

Becoming one in a very sensual way

Melanin glowing

Silk smooth and wet with pleasure

Our sexual choreography

Causing moans to harmonize

Endurance solid

Give and take heightened

Your gyration keeps this ride high vibrational

In sync'd passion keeps this ride euphoric

Exploring you deeper with slight choking

I'm transforming

You're transmitting

I'm rejuvenating

You're enhancing

A sustainability exceeding my expectation

Your muscles tighten around me

Demanding my release

Hand in hand with soft nibbling

My forehead meeting the back of your head

Nectar leaves me seeping through your domain

You face me

Forehead to forehead

Pride filled your face

Peace filled mine

Our souls said yes

Heart rates more calm

Our bodies intertwined

500 Egyptian thread count engulfed us

With a mission well accomplished.

Fruto Prohibido

(Forbidden Fruit)

By way of technology we met

The world wide web

You Puerto Rican

I African American

Vibe and chemistry was different

Passionate

Intense

At such a young age

For me it was taboo

Age…the reason I shouldn't have been touched

I was the forbidden fruit

Your age…my age

The forbidden fruit

Not allowed by law

You in your 40s

I was significantly younger

I was dishonest about my age

Yet honest about my skills

Beautiful beachside home

In less than five minutes

We stood flesh to flesh

Passion ransacked our bodies

I thought I had skills before

Uninhibited and experienced you upgraded them

An animalistic presence came over us

We devoured each other with a very aggressive passion

A very advanced and defined body you had

Just touching you thrilled me more

Nothing on your body had I not tasted before

Yet this was still a first time of sorts

No place on you

My mouth and hands didn't touch and taste

Me having control was fun

You taking control

To a whole different level we went

I was tasted in a way that was pleasingly nasty

My body felt things it never felt

Both stretched to various limits

The way you looked at me

The same passion as when you tasted me

Placing me inside you

Warm and moisture marinated our bodies perfectly

As we became each other's sexual legos

On top

Sideways

Doggystyle

Missionary

No position left unexplored

Age and experience won

As you turned me completely out

Receiving an intoxicated and euphoric high

Too young to understand

Addicted enough to want this feeling more and more

You took all creamy protein my body had to give

Relishing in what just occurred

My real age inquired about

The truth was told

Understanding communicated

Agreements made

More and more occurrences

Chemistry and attachment deep

Segui siendo tu fruta prohibida

You had a hold on me

Desire I never wanted to resist

I was molded

You kept me consistently captivated and saturated with gratification.

Rayda B's Love Notes #4

It wasn't the face and body initially

But yet the spirit, character, and heart

Your love doesn't walk away when it's tough

Mesmerized

Intrigued

I fell hard

It was in the way you touched me

Without using your hands

Remembering your position with me

You ain't my #1

You're my only one

Letting you down…never an option

Deep hurt if you weren't close

Deeper hurt not having you at all

A great foundation intact

Love in the beginning was one part

Us building love 'til the end

A key component

I'm yours

You're mine

No refunds

I found you…I wasn't looking

I questioned was I ready for love

I felt alive again

A risk I had to take

Patient, nurturing, understanding

You amaze me

Wanting to hear about what's circulating in my head

Unafraid…non-judgmental

The miracle I needed badly

More than what I wanted

Everything I never had

You'll keep loving me

I'll keep loving you

The rest will fall in peace.

Rayda B's Love Notes #5

Eight billion people on earth

I only see you

I knew I loved you before we met

My love sees no barriers

It jumps hurdles

Infiltrate walls

Leaps hurdles

A home full of hope and peace

You love me deeply

I love you madly

We love each other unconditionally

Forever and always

You and me everyday

Wanting each other forever

A lot of people caught my eye

Only you caught my heart

Looking beyond what my eyes want

Loving who my heart wants

Other's opinion null and void

My love is yours not theirs

I'll never skip the chance to say I love you

We never skip a chance to show it

I am completely and unconditionally loved

Things come up on which we disagree

We agree to never give up

Keeping secrets

Protecting weaknesses

You smile at me and my soul dances

No matter near or far

Here, there, or anywhere

Our destination is always…love.

Shade, Lip Service, Tasty Treat

Frequent banter

Shady commentary

Our usual mode of communication

A few years younger than I

Small town

Multiple folks in common

I'd yearned and lusted from afar

Thoughts and desires hidden

Details of you unknown

For me some tension

Sexual, sensual, intrigue

Content with lusting in my head

Plethora of body rockin' occurrences

Etched in my fantasies

Smooth caramel skin

Slick mouth that irked and turned me on simultaneously

Lips lookin' like they were made by the purest milk and honey

Glowing and moist to perfection

Personality and laugh that weakened me

Then spontaneity on a cold Brevard night in December

Craving satisfied

My expectation exceeded…

Home

Black leather coach my resting place

Facebook inbox called my name

It was you

I smiled

Nervous, curious, interested

Fun banter, slick mouth, and confidence

A question

My mouth the subject

A comment of its skills given

Like a boomerang you gave it back

You offered your presence

No doubt I quickly obliged

Less than 10

With deliciousness, swag, and appeal

Inside my domain you stood

Dimly lit…ready to show and prove

My bedroom welcoming you

My queen size playground receiving you

Your vision restricted by my tie

Tied around your head

My arousal increased by your lack of hesitation

Whispering don't move…you obeyed

Retrieving something from my kitchen…I returned

I disrobed

Marveling at your smell and smooth skin

Two ice cubes placed in my mouth

Slowing tasting you

Hand gripping your waist

Preventing you from moving

You're stuck

Chills so magnet

I felt them run through your body and into mine

Legs on my shoulders

I tasted you more

Fantasy fulfilled with each motion of my head

You fed my mouth satisfying all appetite and cravings

One hang gripping the sheets

The other the back of my head

Positions changed as you removed the blind fold

Aggressive…like I like it…you pulled my head into yours

Mouth to mouth

Blessed by the taste of you

Hand roaming each other forcefully yet sensually

Lips still locked

Muscles tensed

Veins erect

From our crowns to our toes tips

Our mouths roamed every part of each other's flesh

Leaving no area untasted

None unpleased

Bodies intertwined

A release is near

It's noticed

Rudely you disconnected

My hormones skyrocketed

The tables have turned

Mushed downward on my back

Your look telling me don't move

It's your turn

You're in charge

My look telling you

Your wish is my command

I'm blindfolded

I'm your hurdle ready to be jumped

Your buffet ready to be sampled

Your highway ready to be traveled.

It's The Love For Me

A faulty faith in dreams was strengthened

No believing that dreams can come true

Mine did when I met you

Swearing to always love you

I thought I'd met you with my eyes

We actually met with our souls

I love you to the point where words ain't enough

When I least expected

Your love for me transformed my ordinary life

Into an unprecedented fairy tale

Loving you

Realizing I missed you since before I knew you

A true partnership

You're willing to put in the work needing to build trust

I make myself worthy of it

One promise at a time

You reached out for the darkest and deepest part of me

Wanting the parts that I was hesitant to share

Reminded why I love you so much

A dreamed love

You came and rescued me

With you on this journey

There's no one better I'd rather be with

I'm not fond of my vulnerability

This you know very much

You love me in a very special way

Giving me a safe place and such

The best part of my day

Is having you in my arms

The hardest part of my day

Is being away from you

I fell for you

And you surely caught me

Letting you love me

Like I've never been loved before

At times I feel like your love

Sets off fireworks in my heart

I wonder if people can see

How my love for you just flashes through my skin

Our love isn't about the hugs, kisses, or words shared

It's about the chills that strike my spine

Every time I think of you

Every time I'm near you

Every day and every moment

Do it all over and I'd still choose you.

My Moon, My Heart, My Forever

My sun, my moon, all of my stars you are

Love doesn't care if one is ready

It has its own timeline

To it our hearts adjusted

I fell in love with someone

Who deserved my heart

Not someone to play with it

I deserve folks in my life

To make me feel happy and at peace

Both with me and themselves

From the day I met you

No other soul was worth thinking about

Every single second

My love for you multiplies

I fell in love with you

In a hopeless place

In a mysterious way

The touch of your hand

It intoxicates me

It excites you

It puts me in a frame of mind

Where things seem perfect to me

I find myself longing for your attention

Love at first sight

The thought of it

Ridiculous and funny to me

You came along and stole my heart

Because of you

My faith in HIM increased exponentially

I laugh a lot harder

Cry a lot less

Smile a lot more

Envisioning your face makes my heart race

Falling in love with you.

Makes me second guess

Why I thought being alone was better

A plan

An objective

Never stop making memories with you

If I had a dollar for

Every time I thought of you

Only one I'd have

For you never left my mind

Forever and a day

After the end of it all

When it's all said and done

My heart does and will always belong to you.

Tailor Made

Loving you I was made to do

I love you

No one can change that

Not even time

Never having to force

What's meant to be mine

I flowed to you freely

I know I was made for you

You were made for me

A perfect custom fit souls

Tailor-made bodies

Every time I see you walk

My heart speeds up

I smile

Life is better with us together

Being with you

Rather wet dream, day dream, or a vision

You're a prophecy

Truly a dream come true

Beautiful, tender, strong

Any day with you

Is always one of the best days of my life

In all the world you're the only one that matters

Loving you makes me feel lucky to be alive

In a sea full of people

My eyes will always find you

I'm never not thinking of you

I look at you

The rest of my life is in front of my eyes

You're the last thought when I sleep

The first thought when I wake up

The way you love me

No one else could make me feel

As loved and happy as you do

Jumped hurdles to tell you I loved you

Bravery

You embraced and accepted me

Flaws and all

Falling in love with you

Was as if I walked through a door

And finally felt like I had a home

I look to stare and you're already staring

A dope feeling

The heart wants what it wants

It's logical and rational that it would want you

You're my one love, one heart, one life

Our love is the only emotion that makes me

Brave, scared, weak, and strong all at once

Held hostage

An emotional captive…willingly

Your voice is my favorite sound

You fought for me and made me feel worth it

Consistently my rock

Gratitude

You've been my rainbow after every storm

Refusing to believe I've loved anyone before you

Romance and trust

You hold my heart

Respecting and protecting it at all costs

An amazing feeling

Unexplainable

You see me for who I am

End result – you love me even more

Your love is my love

My love is your love

It's us we fell in love with

It's us we're still in love with

It's us we'll keep loving until the end of time.

Power Of Our Love

Your weirdness is compatible with mine

Joined together

Our love is enriched

By our mutually satisfying weirdness

It's love

Our true love

With commitment to a future together

Cheating is never an option or thought

A relationship truly determined by our hearts

We don't love each other the way we want to

Me and you love each other

The way the other needs to be loved

It wasn't about the love in the beginning

Rather the love we're continuously building

Accountability is a must

Not distracted by blame

Blame is the water that drowns a relationship

We don't just have a relationship with someone we love

But one that has helped us love ourselves more

Memories and photographs captures priceless moments

Reminding us to love as hard as we can

As long as we can

In all the ways that we can

We love hard and unconditionally

Unwavering acceptance

A foundation sparked by real friendship

With the world being tough

Our love is sustained as a safe haven

Never having to be begged, chased, or hit with an ultimatum

We're right where we need to be

We're right where we want to be

Captured by passion of another realm

Moving through a life seasoned with love galore

Not the perfect kind

The undeniably irreplaceable unforgettable kind

A love so intertwined non-verbal communication is strong

You hear me when I'm silent

Looking into each other's eyes

We're the reason we smile

I talk freely

You express yourself openly

Pieces fitted together causing excitement for tomorrow

Being our heart's school

Our relationship has taught us a lot

You see me and I see you

There's safety and security

Arguments and differences handled with care

Love, trust, respect, support

An unstoppable force

Protected and undeniable bond

With us we stand face to face

The people we dream of

When our eyes are closed

Are the same individuals we see when our eyes are open

Realness and consistency

Not standing still or stagnant

We learn, develop, and grow

Step by step

Side by side

A powerful love

Magnetic connection

We feel each other's presence without a single touch

You love me and I love you

The good, bad, and indifferent

Flaws and all

Loving all parts

Even what makes us beautifully imperfect

Connected like a chain link fence

We've granted financial stability

We strengthen each other spiritually

We give each other peace and rest emotionally

We ensure each other calmness and protection mentally

In this we know that we have truly been blessed.

Love You Even More

I fell in love

While learning how to love

A little bit more each day

Is it possible to love you even more

You aren't just the person who holds my hand

You hold my heart

My happiness became complete

At times when we're distant

It is not an obstacle - yet

A beautiful reminder of how strong our love is

It isn't real love

Until you share it with the right person

You're everything right in a wrong world

I loved you when feeling like you were perfect

When seeing your flaws I began to love you even more

If you've done something wrong

Tell me

Let me love you anyway

Nothing about you will disappoint me

There's no preconception

I don't want to foresee you

But rather discover you

You have my whole heart

For my whole life

I don't love you out of convenience

Test my love

It's tried and true

I'd love you even if

You didn't love me back the same way

Even if you didn't love me at all

As long as you're happy

I'd love you even more

A Moon Kissed Healing

There was healing that night

And your body was the temple where I found it

Lavender and chamomile enriched my sense of smell

While shea butter ordained the night

Melanin tantalized every sense of touch

The moonlight shining in through open balcony doors

Showed a work of art blessed slightly extra by the creator

Sense of sight was activated times two

Front lobe kisses cascaded downward to your bosom

Sense of taste extremely satisfied

Sensibilities cherished

Neck and nipples extra sensitive

Releasing moans harmonizing with sweet jazz

That escaped through the speakers

My sense of hearing soothed

While provoking more pleasure

As it's the side kick to my sense of taste

Drips of heaven slips through the sides of my mouth

As the entrance to your inner temple is tapped and drilled

My shoulders become your handlebars

As you brace yourself for a journey

No spit or extra lubrication needed

As your natural nectar

Sweet as apple pie

Smoother than butter

Gives just the right amount of fuel for takeoff

Takeoff to a seesaw of emotions

A seesaw of passion

As legs wrapped around my waist

Arms gripping my shoulders and head

Wild would be an understatement for you

And I have no desire to tame you

Our passion a force of intensity and desire

Lips marked territory

Sweat and saliva mixed to make an intoxicating elixir

Drops adorning every part of the bed and bodies

Two beings fitted like a glove

Digging deep with each thrust

Your nails creating its own artwork on my back

With each stroke of worship in and out of your temple

Prayed

Moaned

Screamed

God was summoned

Moaned

Prayed screamed

Moaned

God was summoned again

Hands tightly squeezing your neck

Delirious and in a zone

Our fire and desire elevated us to a euphoric realm

A place where named are lost

And surroundings forgotten

A high making us consumed by heavenly anointed pleasure

With a release so strong our souls were resuscitated

Senses on high alert

There was a healing that took place that night

A transformative healing

Sexual exorcism

Us baptized in melanin richness.

Do Me Like It Do

It's evident in the way you love me

Just how your love do me like it do

This is beyond flaws, scars, and all

I do not aim to be your favorite or best

I want to be your one and only

While you forget the rest

My smartness doesn't matter

You kiss me and all intelligence goes out the window

I often even forget my own name

Couldn't have anticipated the time or place

It was accidental

It happens in a single flash and heartbeat

In a throbbing moment your love took over me

When you looked at me that night

I fell in love with the expression in your eyes

There was a calm nurturing power you possessed

It increased my courage to love

It isn't just the butterflies I feel

I feel the whole jungle of animals in my stomach

My happiness makes you happy

My sadness makes you sad

In a weak moment you're the strength I need

You're my bridge over the stormy seas of misfortune

My bridge over troubled waters

A spark in the dark

I've met a lot of people

You're the one that changed me forever

There's no need for paradise

I found you

There's no need for dreams

I already have you

You bring out the best in me

With our sweet love

I promise here and now

To give you the best that I got

Climbing mountains

Swimming seas

The calmness soothing any chaos

The sunshine alleviating any storm

Confidence

Assurance

I don't need to look at the stars to dream

Nor make a wish by blowing out candles

Just one look in your eyes

I have what I need

I feel what I need to feel

I see what I need to see

Clear vision and plan made clear

You love me for all that I am

All that I've been

All that I've yet to be

Thinking only God could love unconditionally

You've shown me what it can truly mean

We have a no boundaries kind of love

It is impenetrable

If I could grab a star

Every time you made me smile

If I could grab a planet

Every time you made me feel loved

I'd have the whole universe in the palm of my hand

You have all of my heart and soul

I found my missing piece the day I met you

I'm happy and complete

A better person you've made me with all that you do.

Heart 2 Heart

I go to bed at night

Wishing the day lasted longer

I've clearly spent the day with the right person

If I spend the rest of my life loving you

My life still would not be long enough

I knew I was in love

When certain songs made sense

I don't listen to the voices of other people

I listen to my heart

Submitted to it never steers me wrong

You are the smile on my face

You are the beat in my heart

I don't need sunshine nor anything to do

When I'm with you

A rainy day seems like a holiday

You've brought sunshine to all my storms

Ignoring who I thought I wanted you to be

I'm loving you for who you are

When I fell in love with you

I gave you the right to hurt me

Yet trusting that you'd never tear me apart

Your heart is the only one for me

My love is the only one for you

You took my heart and decided to keep it

For me there's no greater love

Being always on my mind

And embedded in my spirit

Falling in love with you was easy

Having you in my life

Makes me not want to go to sleep

You've made my reality

Far better than any dream

I smell you from down the street

And sense you from a mile away

In a crowded room

A start among stars

I'll always find you

High, low, near, or far

You are my blue crayon

The color I can't get enough of

With pride I use you to color my sky

I did the work and healed it's true

I fell in love with myself first

So that I could find my way to you.

I Love You I Do

Me being with you

Is as peaceful as a midsummer night's dream

Calm and serenity

Tranquility and a romantic reverence

I'd give you everything

Expecting nothing in return

I love you I do

My soulmate

You don't just kiss my lips

You kiss my soul

No distance too great between us

Hearts intertwined truly loving each other

Your love gives me freedom

Whether I need to

Laugh, cry, sing, dance, scream

I am just simply loved

With you I'm never afraid

Our love is a friendship on fire

Pretty, fierce, hot

Growing and sustaining

Become as unquenchable and deep burning as coal

I love you I do

To the world you'd just be one person

To me you're the entire world in one person

I love who you're becoming

I love who you are

I love who you were

I love you I do

Our love created an us

Without destroying a me

My love for you is selfish

I can't breathe without you

This love thing is natural when I'm with you

The electricity from us lights up a room

I love you without imposing desires

We're completely free, limitless, and selfless

Whenever your body touches mine

I am home

Your inner and outer is like the leaves of autumn

Consistently changing and always beautiful

Our love is wild and passionate

Never mediocre

You're my happily ever after

Our story is my favorite love story

Our love did not occur between two perfect people

It occurred between two people perfect for each other

We trust each other with our most valuable possession

Our heart

Souls are eternal

You've had a piece of mine from the beginning

Our love is any, even though, in spite of

When I wake in the morning and contemplate life

I look at you

I smile

Joy and assurance

Everything in life falls into place

Everything 'bout life makes sense

That's why I love you I do.

My Love, Your Love, Our Love

Yes it's messy

Yet it's the story that got us here

I love our love story

You far exceeded any expectation

Of what I thought love was

Starting at eternity and ending at never

Our love story is a journey

My soulmate

It's all in my love, your love, our love

You are my wildest adventure and my safest home

I was unaware of the magnitude and capacity of my love

Until I fell in love with you

My hobby is missing you

My job is caring for you

My duty is making you happy

For forever my life is loving you

I keep falling for you and never want to recover

Your charm captivates me since the first time eyes met

For I love you not because of anything you have

It's because of what I feel when I'm near you

It's all in my love, your love, our love

I found love with you

I walked away from what I didn't love

I removed myself from what I didn't need

You are the miracle I needed so bad

You are the best thing that's happened to me

When I tell you I love you

No habit

No routine

A reminder

A show and tell

Of how you mean the world to me

Relationships are worth fighting for

Neither one of us are fighting alone

Respect

Understanding

Appreciation

Acceptance

It's all in my love, your love, our love

Our love story is rare

My happiest moods

My biggest smiles

Occur whenever I'm near you

The only battle I'm happy losing

Is the one against unconditional love

If our love is a dream

Let me never be woken

If our love is real

I never want to sleep again.

Rayda B's Love Notes #6

Without a shadow of a doubt

I will never unlove you

I've found love

I cherish you

It is real

Awareness

Our type of love is hard to find

I did not see love

I found it

We are best friends and lovers

Two souls instantly connecting

Knowing the wait is over at last

Yesterday, today, tonight, tomorrow, forever

You'll always be in my heart

To it you hold the key

With my whole world in your arms

You on my chest after a bad day

Everything made better

Fully in love

I love every version of you

Sad, angry, happy, sassy, funny

I love all of them

Due to loving all of you

Unplanned true love has been

The gift that keeps on giving

You love me for no reason

You make it a priority to shower me with reasons

There's an ultimate happiness you receive

There's an ultimate bond that's deepened

With us words aren't necessary

Our hearts speak to each other

Heart to heart

Our hearts have a language all their own

Not a day goes by

Where I reminisce about you

Reminisce how you care for me

I'm lucky, favored, blessed

Many times thinking God had forgotten about me

That true love wasn't his plan…for me

I met you

Everything was well worth the wait

I am the whole of your heart

You are the center of my world

We are the source of our joys

Our love is a friendship that caught on fire

It's mutually confident with

Sharing and forgiving

Guided by a quiet understanding

Good or bad we're loyal

Connected and bonded together forever and beyond

No distance is too far

No time too long

No other force can break us apart.

Loving Me, Loving Deep, Loving Self

I am enough

You can think what you want

I don't stress about it

Self-aware

Knowing the truth

Truth made known by those who love me

Is it too late

Just now realizing how dope I am

Will I be great

Loving myself fully

If no one else does

Not important

Carries no weight

Owning my strength and power

Wearing it proudly

Not dimming my light

Not diminishing my weight

Just so you feel comfortable

I deserve more love

Always did

Always will

Loving myself unconditionally

Not quick to fall in love

Not forgetting to love myself first

If all I do is love myself more

Today was great

Being the prize

Not chasing anyone

Not needing you to complete me

Needing you to remind me

Of my amazingness that already exists

Not letting someone

Not worth my love

Causing forgetfulness of my worth

I'm giving myself the love I seek

Trusting that HE

Will send people who match it

Acceptance

Loving myself

1st step to self-love

Pouring love into myself

Smile becomes bigger each day

I am not perfect

I am a work of art

Embracing imperfections

Loving myself a bit harder each day

Loving myself enough

Time and efforts

Makes dreams a reality

Folks I've come across

Cherished

Folks have loved, liked, accepted

No matter the mood

Amazingness still exists

Deserving the love and attention I give to you

Following my heart to the life I've dreamed about

Dating myself

Spoiling myself

Falling in love with myself

Loving myself and striving for bigger

One day at a time

Ceased trying to make you understand me

Living life happy – no discrimination

Those who loving me…solid… no explanation.

Loving You Long Time

Many have caught my eye

A certain specialness to catch my heart

Waiting wasn't always easy

Loving while waiting

Is an enjoyable thing

You possess this uniqueness

Very much amazing

You were strong enough to wait

For what you deserve

I was man enough to realize it from the start

The way you love me

Makes me love myself more

I leave the light on in my heart

So that whenever you're lost

You'll find your way back home

A reflection of you

You changed my ways

You change my life

My mind thinks of you

My eyes see you

My heart loves you

My feet walk to you

My hands comfort you

My mouth pleases you

My spirit prays for you

Minutes feel like years when we're apart

Hours like seconds when we're together

Loving you deeply

Gratefully

Not for what you are

It's for who I've become

By being with you

How did I deserve you

You love me loudly

Proudly

Publicly

With you I'm able to lower the guard

Being truer

Being vulnerable

You accept and love me all the same

This started as a lil' somethin' somethin'

This is a love thang

The real deal

The Denzel and Pauletta

The Cardi and Offset

The Ruth and Boaz

Barak and Michelle

I love you and will always love you

Until I die

And in the after life

I'll still be loving you then

Whether a mansion with millions

A studio and a dime

I'll always be loving you long time.

Pulse, Pressure, Pleasure

Our pleasure shouldn't have happened

You belonged to someone else

We became each other's best kept secret

Our experiences were heaven to us

If known – looked down upon

College

Friends

Connections

Greek life

Same council – different colors

Our commonalities

Dirty south engulfed with a Philly Native

Met by chance

Friend of a friend

Immediate and infectious

Side looks

Stolen glances

Behind the back conversations

Greek event attended

Left early

Different doors our exit

No need to use the key card

Door already cracked

Dimly lit

Smell of Rouge filled the room

Slowly disrobing as I walked to make a drink

Liquid courage

Intrigued

Excited

Liquid intoxication to a sensual intoxication

Sipped D'usse

Smelled you close

I felt you

Fenty to Fenty

Face to face

Eye to eye

My drink indulged slowly

You tasted me

Hormones and liquor

A traveling fool rushing through my body

Guided to the bed

Back down

Spread eagle

I was explored

I was your road map

Your lips and tongue traveled me

Left right

Up down

In out

Reciprocation not allowed

Movement restricted

I am the willing victim of your desire

My pulse heightened

Staccato beats

Pressure applied in the right places

Eyes rolled back

Muscles tensed

Penetration acceleration

Exploration

Destination

Your pleasure and joy elevated by my enjoyment

No part of me or you

Not touched, tasted, stretched, savored, nourished

We salivated, designated, ejaculated

Pillow talk accompanied an intermission

Liquid fuel

The dark kind

Rejuvenation

Time for an encore

A finale revisited more than once afterwards

An expert you became

Hands on my pulse

An addition to the pressure applied

Hypnotized by your sexual stimulation

Unprecedented pleasure invariably satisfied.

About The Author

Ra'Mone Marquis is a southern gentleman, born and raised in the sunshine state of Florida. Life experiences and literary idols such as Omar Tyree, Terry McMillan, and Eric Jerome Dickey; have shaped Ra'Mone into the author that he is today. This is what formed the foundation of him being a refreshing literary artist with high levels of uniqueness and relatability.

Seeing a need in his community, specifically with that of minority youth, Ra'Mone started his 501c3 foundation – Tru Phoenix Foundation, Inc. (formerly known as True T.A.L.E.N.T.S. Foundation, Inc.). Since its inception in 2011, this foundation has served a plethora of minority youth in the central and south Florida areas through its mentoring conference, mentoring sessions, and various initiatives.

Courtesy of his company Tru Phoenix, LLC., formally Kace Books, LLC., he has released 5 written works. They are all 5-star reviewed and 4 have reached the Amazon Bestsellers List. They are District 69: The Crimson Edition, District 69:

The Color Haven, District 69: The Greek Chronicles, his first #1 book A Poetic Exhale, and Ice Box: Rebound & Recover. All books are available on Kindle, Amazon, ibooks, and his website (www.ramonemarquisofficial.com).

Ra'Mone is also the host of his own podcast, The QB Zone. All episodes are available on iheartradio, Spotify, Apple Podcasts, Google Podcasts, and Amazon Music; video episodes available on his YouTube channel: Quis Box.